ANTS

INSECTS DISCOVERY LIBRARY

Jason Cooper

Rourke Publishing LLC
Vero Beach, Florida 32964

www.rourkepublishing.com

PHOTO CREDITS: Cover, p. 4, 10 (large), 15 © James H. Carmichael; title page, p. 9, 10 (inset), 13, 16 (both), 21, 22 © Alex Wild; p. 7, 8, 18 © Lynn M. Stone

Title page: Orange army ants attack a black ant as they raid a nest.

Library of Congress Cataloging-in-Publication Data

Cooper, Jason, 1942-
  Ants / Jason Cooper.
     p. cm. -- (Insects discovery library)
  Includes bibliographical references.
  ISBN 1-59515-424-8 (hardcover)
  1. Ants--Juvenile literature. I. Title.
  QL568.F7C776 2006
  595.79'6--dc22
                                2005010967

Printed in the USA

Rourke Publishing

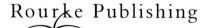

www.rourkepublishing.com – sales@rourkepublishing.com
Post Office Box 3328, Vero Beach, FL 32964
1-800-394-7055

TABLE OF CONTENTS

Ants   5
Where Ants Live   11
Being an Ant   12
Ant Food   17
Young Ants   20
Glossary   23
Index   24
Further Reading/Websites to Visit   24

Ants

Ants all have six legs, which means they are **insects**.

There are more than 8,000 kinds of ants. Most are very small. The largest ants are just 1 inch (2.5 centimeters) long.

A harvester ant shows its mouth.

Ants live together in **colonies**. Each ant in a colony has a job to do. Worker ants collect food. Ants often share jobs.

Ants live and work together in colonies.

Many ants have a **stinger**. An ant's stinger is at the far end of its body. Wasps and bees also have stingers.

The ant stinger can really hurt you.

Bees and wasps are relatives of ants.

Weaver ants make their nests in leaves.

Where Ants Live

Ants may be found almost anywhere on dry land.
Ants live underground. They live in dirt mounds.
Ants live under tree bark. Some kinds live in attics.

Most ants are brown or black.

11

Being an Ant

Ants are small, but they are strong. One ant can lift the weight of perhaps 30 other ants! Can you lift 30 classmates?

A worker honeypot ant moves a queen.

Ants lead amazing lives. Some kinds guard other insects like **aphids**. The aphids make food for the ants.

A leaf-cutter ant lifts a leaf and several worker ants.

An ant drinks a drop of honeydew from an aphid.

Ant Food

Some kinds of ants attack other animals for food. Different kinds of ants eat different foods. Army ants eat insects. Some ants eat seeds or food crumbs. Others eat dead animals or aphid **honeydew**.

Aphids make honeydew for ants.

Ants are eaten by many animals. Lizards love ants. What do you think anteaters eat?

Did You Know?

Many ants stay in or close to their nests.

A horned lizard has found an ant colony.

Young Ants

Only the queen ant lays eggs. The babies that hatch look like worms. They are called **larva**.

In time the larva change into another stage of life. This is called the **pupa**. The pupa changes into an adult ant.

A trap-jaw ant gently moves a larva in the nest.

Did You Know?

Fire ants in the southern United States eat crops and small animals.

GLOSSARY

aphids (AY fidz) — tiny insects that eat plants

colonies (KOL uh neez) — groups of insects that live and
   work together

honeydew (HUN ee DYU) — a sweet liquid made by some
   insects, like aphids

insects (IN SEKTZ) — small, boneless animals with six legs

larva (LAR vuh) — a stage of an insect's life before it becomes
   an adult

pupa (PYU puh) — the quiet, final stage of life for some insects
   before they become adults

stinger (STING ur) — a small but sharp organ that causes a sting

*Fire ants swarm
over a grasshopper.*

INDEX

aphids   14

colonies   6

eggs   20

food   14, 17

honeydew   17

insects   5

larva   20

lizards   19

pupa   20

stinger   9

Further Reading

Gomel, Luc. *Face-to-Face with the Ant*. Charlesbridge, 2001

Hodge, Deborah. *Ants*. Kids Can Press, 2004

Websites to Visit

http://www.worldalmanacforkids.com/explore/animals/ant.html

http://www.zoomschool.com/subjects/insects/ant/

About the Author

Jason Cooper has written many children's books for Rourke Publishing about a variety of topics. Cooper travels widely to gather information for his books.